THE BUNGLING

"You're not going out," said Mrs Green.
"Yes, I am going out," said Mr Green.
"But it's my birthday!"
"It's going to be a good night."
"No! You're not going out on my birthday!"

A big row was going on at 43 Villa Road.
Yes, a very big row was going on at 43 Villa Road.
Mrs Green was having a row with Mr Green.
Mr Green was a burglar.

"You're not going out on my birthday!"
Mrs Green yelled.
"Yes, I am going out. I'm a burglar."
Mrs Green was very cross with Mr Green.
She went out of the sitting-room and got a big pan.
She was that cross.

Mrs Green came back in the sitting-room with the pan.
"You're not going out on my birthday," she said.
"But, darling, it's going to be a good night to burgle."
"Don't darling me!" she yelled.
She hit Mr Green with the big pan.

"Look what you've done!" yelled Mr Green. "Look what you've done! You've broken my glasses."
"Good, now you can't go out," she said.
"Yes, I can," said Mr Green, "I'm going out to burgle."

"But you won't see without glasses,"
said Mrs Green. "You'll get caught.
The police will get you."
"No, I won't get caught. I'm a good burglar."
"You'll get caught without your glasses," she said.

"I'll bring back presents for your birthday,"
said Mr Green.
"I don't want presents. You're not going out."
She was very cross!
"Yes, I am going out," said Mr Green.
And he went out of the house and down the road.

It was very dark out in the road.
He could not see well without his glasses in the dark.
Then he heard a police car.
Mr Green ran down the road.

He ran and ran in the dark, round and round.
He could not tell where he was without his glasses.
Then he saw a house.
It could be full of silver and 'presents' for
Mrs Green.
He crept down the path of the house.

What luck! He could just see that it had a burglar alarm like his.
He could fix that and get in the house.
He got up to it.
Yes, he could just see it to fix it.
Then he crept round the back of the house.

What luck! Round the back it had windows just like his.
He could get in windows like that.
He could fix windows like that and get in.
Yes, he crept round the house.

But there was a dog in the house.
It ran up to him. It ran round and round him.
Mr Green shook with fright.
But it did not bark, it licked him.
Yes, it was going to be a good night for 'presents' for Mrs Green's birthday.

He crept in the sitting-room of the house.
He shone his torch round the room.
He could just see a cupboard full of silver.
What luck! What good 'presents' for Mrs Green.
It was a good night to burgle.

He put the silver in his bag.
The dog came up and ran round and round him.
Then it licked him. It did not bark as he went to the window.
Burglar Green crept out of the window with his bag full of silver.

Back at 43 Villa Road Mrs Green sat up in bed.
Someone was getting in the window of No 43.
Someone had crept in the sitting-room.
And Mr Green was not home yet.
She shook with fright.

What a birthday! What a birthday! Mr Green out and someone in the house.
She shook with fright as she heard someone in the sitting-room.
Their house was being burgled.
Their house was being burgled when Mr Green was out!

Mr Green crept down the path of the house he had burgled.
Then he heard a police car.
Mr Green ran and ran in the dark. He went round and round with the bag full of silver.
When he stopped he could not tell where he was without his glasses.

He could just see the gate of a house.
He shone his torch on the house. What luck!
No 43.
It was his house. Yes, it was a good night.

He went down the path of his house.
He went in the door.
In the house his dog came up and licked him.
He went up to his wife with his 'presents'.

19

But she yelled at him.
"We've been burgled. We were burgled when you were out. Someone crept in the window of the house. Someone was in the sitting-room. I shook with fright."

"Darling," said Mr Green to Mrs Green, "look what I've got for your birthday. Just for you. 'Presents'."
He took the silver out of the bag and put it on the bed.

"You bungling burglar!" she yelled. "It's our silver out of the cupboard! Without your glasses on you've burgled your own house. What a bungling burglar you are!"

22

Mr Green went down to the sitting-room.
The dog came up and licked him.
He had burgled his own house.
He could see his silver was not in the cupboard.
He was a bungling burglar.

Then Mr Green heard a police car come up to the house.
"The police!" he yelled.
"Yes, I phoned the police," said Mrs Green. "I said someone had got in the house. What a birthday! You bungling burglar!"